bread
of blessing,
cup of
hope

bread
of blessing,
cup of
hope

Prayers at the
Communion Table

by Michael E. Dixon

CHALICE
PRESS

ST. LOUIS, MISSOURI

Biblical quotations unless otherwise noted, are from the *New Revised Standard Version of the Bible,* copyright 1989, Division of Christian Education of the National Council of Churches of Christ in the USA. Used by permission.

Cover: RSR Associates

www.chalicepress.com

18   17   16   15   12   13   14   15   16

Library of Congress Cataloging–in–Publication Data

Dixon, Michael E.
    Bread of blessing, cup of hope / by Michael E. Dixon
      p.   cm.
    ISBN 978-0-827204-50-8
    Includes index.
    1. Lord's Supper—Prayer-books and devotions—English.
    I. Title
  BV826.5.D59   1987   87-15839
  264'.36

Printed in the United States of America

Introduction

Before other worshipers have gathered, dedicated people have prepared the elements and set them in their place at the Lord's Table. The bread and cup now remind the worshipers of an invitation from their Christ and God to come and eat, come and drink, come and be in communion. It is a special place, a special time. It is part memory and part hope, part refreshment and part challenge, part routine and part mystery. Each person gathered, around the table or in the pews, is not just a spectator, but a participant in a drama enacted in symbol and deed, word and thought.

When the invitation is extended, a hymn sung, and the words of institution spoken, that special place is full of silent prayer—some joyous and celebrative, some quiet, some—from the depths of pain—aided by the Spirit "with sighs too deep for words" (Romans 8:26). In the midst of that quiet symphony of prayer come the spoken prayers—the expressed prayers of the community of faith. What a responsibility, what a privilege, to be one of those called upon to pray at the Lord's Table!

Bread of Blessing, Cup of Hope is offered as an aid, a sourcebook, for those given that responsibility and privilege. The prayers here can serve as models, promptings, or clues to give a leader input in preparation of his or her prayers. If they stimulate your thoughts, sharpen your insights, and focus your attention, they will serve their purposes.

How should one use this book? One helpful way would be to choose a set of prayers for reading in private meditation before each Sunday's service, whether one is to pray publicly in that service or not. Use the prayers in preparation of the heart as well as the tongue. Read with a pen in hand. Underline. Write your own variations in the margins. Question. When you have chosen a prayer, read it prayerfully, then pray in your own words. Be still and quiet awhile. Then write your own prayer.

How should you choose a particular prayer? There are several options:

* Use whichever prayer speaks to you meaningfully at a given point.

* Use the references to the seasons of the church year, if your service of worship follows those patterns. Many congregations use the seasons of the church year as a way to provide balance and flow to their worship life. If yours is one, it shouldn't be too difficult to find which Sundays of the church year are your Sundays to serve.

* Use the scriptural index on the last pages of this book. Do any of the scripture passages that are being read in the service appear there? Look up the prayers with those references, using the number on the upper-right corner of each page.

Finally, as you use this book, you might want to know what elements shaped its format and thought. Here are some of those elements.

* *A belief that the service of worship should have wholeness and integrity, and that each element of the service should have both interrelatedness and integrity.* Communion prayers shouldn't try to be pastoral prayers, but they can carry forth the predominant themes of the service. They can help set the communion service into the context of what has come before and what comes after.

* *An attempt to be responsive to the flow of the church year.* Although a prayer is labeled "Second Sunday of Lent," it can be used at other times when it might seem appropriate. Each

prayer is informed by the scripture readings assigned for that particular Sunday by the New Common Lectionary. Each prayer also is informed by the general themes of a given season of the church year.

* Related to that, *an affirmation that the language of prayer begins in scripture.* The story in the Bible and our stories, God's revealed grace and actions, and our needs—all find a meeting point in scripture and prayer.

* *An attempt to be sensitive to contemporary language and theology, while staying within the great traditions of the church.* We are part of a total human community and need to be sensitive to all our brothers and sisters in Christ. In practice, this means these prayers won't refer to "man," "mankind," or "brotherhood" in the generic sense. In theology, this means that God is beyond human distinctions of male and female, as God is beyond all metaphors we use in speaking of God. Yet because God is beyond definition, metaphors are all we have. In these prayers, I most often address God simply as God, and use a wide variety of metaphors, almost all of them biblical. Context has determined their use—thus a few male-specific references will be found, as they best fit a given context.

Through the years of my life—as a child, youth, student, pastor, and elder in a local congregation, I have come to the Lord's Table and heard many prayers there—some simple in word and idea, and others more finely stated. Yet common to all the prayers was one important thing—the devotion, love, and spirituality of those who prayed them. These believers, ranging from those who never finished grade school to those who have earned doctorates, have taught me that it isn't the wording of the prayers that matters as much as the love for Jesus Christ and the church that was expressed as the words were spoken. To these people who have blessed the bread and cup, and blessed my life, I dedicate this book.

For Personal Preparation

My sisters and brothers in Christ are gathering to worship you, dear God. By your gracious calling I will be helping them worship by serving at your table. In some ways this frightens me because I don't always feel worthy for your service. Help calm me and center me. Center my heart and focus my mind. Guide my words and actions, that glory may be yours. Let me trust not in my own abilities, but in your grace, for that is always sufficient. I pray to you, my God, through Christ, my Savior. Amen.

For Personal Preparation

God, you have called me to a significant responsibility in the life of our church. Help me fulfill the role and functions of eldership in such a way that you will say, "Well done, good and faithful servant." Although I often feel personally unworthy, I know that you can take the clay of human weakness and turn it to the gold of Christian service.

I remember now other elders, men and women, who have served as role models for me. I thank you especially for _____ , and _____ , and their special ministry to the church and to me.

Guide my life in the way of faithfulness, as you guided theirs, that the prayers I give at the table may be the natural extensions of the prayers I live in my daily life. I pray in the name of Jesus the Christ, who is the Way, the Truth, and the Life for me. Amen.

A Service of Communion

For Use in Hospitals, Nursing Homes, and Private Homes

CALL TO WORSHIP: Although we cannot attend a worship service in our church building today, we can still affirm that we are a part of our community of faith, that we are bonded together in Christian love and prayers with all our family of faith, and that wherever two or three are gathered together, Christ is with us. This service of communion we are about to share is a witness that God is here, that Christ is here, that the church is here. Come, let us worship God in the beauty of holiness.

Let us now hear the words of a psalm. (*The elder may read the following selection or one from the list following this service.*) I will sing of thy steadfast love, O Lord, for ever; with my mouth I will proclaim thy faithfulness to all generations. For thy steadfast love was established for ever, thy faithfulness is firm as the heavens (*Psalm 89:1-2*).

Let us join our hearts in prayer: As we worship you here today, dear God, we thank you for the love we have received through Jesus Christ, a love symbolized so beautifully by this bread and cup. Let it remind us of Jesus Christ, that he lived and died and rose again and, through your Spirit, lives in us today. Let this bread and cup remind us of the church, for we

13

share not alone but as members one of another. Let this communion be a sign of the hope and promise we have of new life in the kingdom of God. As we share these elements, we remember in prayer . . . (*here, the elder may offer the names of others with special needs, the pastor, or other church leaders*). We pray now that _____ (*name of the person or persons being served*) here will know our love and concern and that (he/she/they) will feel your healing, helping presence. Hear our prayer in Jesus' name. Amen.

Let us hear the words of institution: Now as they were eating, Jesus took bread, and blessed, and broke it, and gave it to the disciples and said, "Take, eat; this is my body." And he took a cup, and when he had given thanks he gave it to them, saying, "Drink of it, all of you; for this is my blood of the covenant, which is poured out for many for the forgiveness of sins" (*Matthew 26:26-27*). (*Now the bread and the cup may be served.*)

God be with you. I will keep you in my prayers this week, and I ask that you keep me in yours. Now may the peace that passes all understanding keep your hearts and minds in Christ Jesus, our Lord. Amen.

Additional Psalms That Can Be Read

Psalm 8
Psalm 23
Psalm 27:1, 4-5, 13-14
Psalm 42:1-5
Psalm 62:1-2
Psalm 67

Psalm 84:1-4
Psalm 91:1-2
Psalm 100
Psalm 116:1-7
Psalm 139:1-6
Psalm 147:1-3

Additional Words of Institution

Mark 14:22-25
John 6:35
1 Corinthians 11:23-26

First Sunday of Advent

For the Bread

In our yesterdays, O God, you watched us and protected us while we were helpless infants. In our todays, amidst the frantic confusion of a busy time in a hectic land, you are the still center of silence and strength. In our tomorrows, you are the only true source of hope and the destination of all our wanderings. At this table we pause to reflect upon the Christ who was, who is, and who evermore shall be. With this bread, we proclaim that our hope is in the meek and self-giving love of Christ, one willing to be broken in body and spirit that we might find wholeness and health. Amen.

1

For the Cup

As we stand at the beginning of the Advent season, O God of hope, we pray for your guidance that we might be aware—our spirits alert, our lives ready for your Word to be born in us again. Let this cup remind us that you were willing to drink from the cup of weak humanity to share the burdens we all must carry, to bleed with us in our hurting places. Help us as we drink of it to become more dedicated to encourage, support, and love one another as you have loved us. In the coming Lord's name we pray. Amen.

Second Sunday of Advent

For the Bread

Our days are being spent in busy preparation for the holidays, our God and Father of Jesus Christ. In these days of preparation, prepare our hearts and spirits for your coming into our lives. Let the bread we break remind us that you are the source of all our life and all our energy. Help us to grow in grace and faith that we might receive the Christ, who is the true goal of all our preparation and anticipation, the Christ who would be the perfect example to guide us in our self-giving love.

2

For the Cup

God of time and eternity, you are always with us, yet always in the process of coming. As we gather at this table of communion, help us to know that you are here, yet help us to wait expectantly for your work and word to be fulfilled in our lives. As we drink of the fruit of the vine, let us be filled with the fruit of righteousness as an expression of your wondrous gift of love in Jesus Christ our Lord. Amen.

Third Sunday in Advent

For the Bread

In our well-fed land, our God and provider, we think of hunger in terms of diets, not deprivation. But while our bodies are well fed, our inner lives hunger for something of more substance. As we eat this loaf, we recall the Christ that was born to be the Bread of Life, humanity's nourishment and joy. Fill us with your gladness; renew us in your love; set us free from all that would oppress and enslave us as we receive the Bread of Life, so that we may share it with others who hunger like us. Amen.

3

For the Cup

As we drink from this small cup, O Creator of hope and joy, we realize that we are drinking spiritually from the wellspring of all joy. We affirm that the refreshment that comes from Christ's presence in our lives is a source of joy that will never run dry. When the world's pleasures would leave us thirsting and joyless, guide us to quench the thirst of our dry spirits here, that we might rise up and sing "Joy to the world. the Lord Is Come!" Amen.

Fourth Sunday in Advent

For the Bread

God of mercy and justice, we come to this table anticipating the coming of Jesus Christ, the Prince of Peace. We want to set aside the fears, rivalries, and hatreds that create terrorism, threat of war, and the agony of war itself. As we eat this bread of life, center our hearts and minds on the paths of peace, reconciliation, justice, and unity that you would have us follow if we are to walk in the paths of Jesus Christ. Amen.

4

For the Cup

When the world calls us to power, you call us to mercy. When the world calls us to conquest, you call us to peace. When the world calls us to lives of acquisition, you call us to lives of sharing. Help us, God of gentleness, to beat our swords into plowshares. Help us discipline our seeking of mercy for ourselves and stern justice for those who have wronged us into the seeking of mercy and peace for all. In this cup we recognize that we have been called into a holy and gentle life through the offering of life that Jesus Christ made for us. Help our lives be transformed by the presence of the Christ Child, that the peace of the manger may become the Peace of the world. Amen.

First Sunday After Christmas

For the Bread

The presents are opened. The relatives have returned home. The vacations and parties are over. O Ruler of our days, it seems that the special times of Christmas have ended. Yet the bread we break now reminds us that Christmas is a beginning, not an ending. The birthday of Jesus was the beginning of his journey of growth, a time to increase in stature, wisdom, and favor in your eyes and in humanity's. And we remember with this celebration of communion where that journey would end—on a cross of pain and suffering. Yet even that was not an ending, but a new beginning, a beginning of the power of the risen Christ in our midst. Let this risen Christ guide us on our life journeys, that we too may grow in wisdom and in your favor. Amen.

5

For the Cup

We come as one people to drink this cup, O gracious and giving God. We come grateful for what this cup represents, the life of our Savior Jesus Christ, which was given that we might have the joy of life abundant. Help us learn at this table to be truly one in love, forgiving one another as you have forgiven us. Help us to dwell in your word always, and to live out your peace in our words, our witness, and our work. Amen.

Second Sunday After Christmas

For the Bread

God, our creator, we find ourselves in a world of change. The slow march of seasons brings change in weather. We grow older, older. Infants are born, and people die. Our society changes at an ever-quickening pace. Yet the still center around which everything turns is you. Your love for us, as revealed in this broken bread and in the broken body of Jesus Christ our Lord, is unchanging, unending, and ever constant. As we eat this bread, let it nourish our spirits. Let this moment of communion anchor our lives to your unchanging love. We pray in Jesus' name. Amen.

6

For the Cup

As we drink this cup, O God of all faithfulness, we seal a covenant: a covenant the prophet said would be written on our hearts. Help us remember this covenant of love when we would falter, when we would compromise, when we would give in to the pressures of life. Help us to be faithful, even as you are faithful and true in your promises through Jesus Christ our Lord. Amen.

Epiphany

For the Bread

God of light, we recall the light of the Christmas star that led travelers across the desert to your glory. We think of the light that came into the world, teaching, healing, calling, and caring. And at the same time we recall the dim light of the upper room when Jesus took the bread, and blessed it, and shared it with the first disciples. Let your light shine in our lives as we share this bread now at your table. Amen.

7

For the Cup

As travelers of old came across the wilderness to
bring gifts to the Christ Child, dear God, so we
stop and rest from our journeys through life and
offer to you gifts of our love. Accept this cup,
and the wine within, as the work of our hands,
and bless it that we might receive it back from
you as a far greater gift—the sign of your love
and grace in Jesus Christ our Lord. Amen.

Second Sunday After Epiphany

For the Bread

Everlasting God, your love is revealed to us in so many ways, if we could but see. Your care holds us close; your protection keeps us safe; your generosity teaches us to share with all human-kind. As we break this bread, we thank you that your loving kindness is best revealed in Jesus Christ our Savior, whose body was broken that we might know wholeness. Teach us to see and perceive your glory revealed to us, and teach us to help make it visible, as a burning torch in a dark world. We pray in the name of the true Light, Jesus Christ. Amen.

8

For the Cup

God of all life, you have invited us to a feast of joy, a celebration of love. At this feast we have been blessed with your presence. For here it is that the water of routine life has been transformed into the wine of experiencing new life in Christ. In drinking this best wine that was saved for last, the wine of Christ's overflowing love, we rejoice because you are here in our midst. Amen.

Third Sunday After Epiphany

For the Bread

We were in darkness; you have given us light.

We were in prisons of fear; you have visited us with hope.

We were stripped of our dignity; you put royal robes on our shoulders.

Now we are hungering and thirsting for righteousness and you have given us this bread.

For answering our deepest needs and prayers with this meal of grace, we thank you, God. Amen.

9

For the Cup

God of Moses, when the Hebrews were thirsting in the wilderness, you had your servant strike a rock, and waters gushed forth.

God of Elijah, on Mount Carmel you broke a drought and demonstrated your power to a faithless people.

God of Jesus Christ, when our spirits longed for you as a deer in the wilderness pants for a flowing stream, you offered us living water.

As we drink this cup, we are refreshed and blessed by Jesus Christ. We thank you, God. Amen.

Fourth Sunday After Epiphany

For the Bread

Creator God, we glimpse your power and majesty in the beauty of the winter skies. We glimpse your providence and care in our rich land. We glimpse your creativity and promise in the face of a newborn child. But it is when we come to this table and break this bread that we see what is most special—your self-sacrificing love for us, your children. Thank you that your love is revealed to us in breaking bread. Amen.

10

For the Cup

We continue in prayer, O God of life, affirming that you sent Jesus to draw us toward life abundant. As we prepare to drink this cup, we remember how your love was revealed in Jesus Christ's witness and words, suffering and sacrifice, in the living Christ, who dwells among us and within. Our cup overflows with goodness and mercy as we share this cup of life. Let your glory be revealed as we pray and meditate. In Jesus' name. Amen.

Fifth Sunday After Epiphany

For the Bread

We come to your table in response to your gracious call, O God of light and life. We come trusting, yet a little frightened, knowing that you can fill our lives to the bursting point with your power, as you once filled the disciples' nets. As we eat this bread of communion, we pray that you will nourish us and enable us to be strong, brave, winsome, and willing. Help us to be fishers of all humanity, vital witnesses for the living Christ, in whose name we gather around this table. Amen.

11

For the Cup

Sometimes we are fearful, O God, of transforming holiness, because our lives seem so pathetic and shabby in comparison with what they might be. We try to live safely, following rules, staying within boundaries, meeting expectations, keeping out of trouble. Then you call us to your service, transforming our whole world. Like Isaiah in the temple, like some fishermen by the Sea of Galilee, like Paul on the road to Damascus, we are confronted by your holy love, by your divine call to service. Let this cup that we share be a symbol of the call to discipleship you offer us and an emblem of your overflowing blessing to those who respond and follow your direction. Amen.

Sixth Sunday After Epiphany

For the Bread

God of wisdom, you are the great teacher. Help us learn your way. Be patient with us when we learn slowly, when we put our trust in our own resources and come to feel dried up and burned out. Invite us again to sink our roots deep into your love. Teach us to find our nourishment in you, as we share in this symbolic act of eating bread, that we may flourish in your spirit like trees beside the living water. In the life-giving name of Christ we come. Amen.

12

For the Cup

God of mercy, we come to this table realizing
that this cup is a strong symbol of your forgiveness and your will to restore us to relationship
with you and with one another. We are weak and
anxious, much like the original disciples at our
Savior's table, struggling with feelings of doubt,
fear, denial, even betrayal. As this cup is passed,
let us realize your power of forgiveness working
in us. Help us find here the strength to live gently
and lovingly, to forgive others as you have
forgiven us, and to accept forgiveness from those
we have wronged. We pray in the name of the
one who sealed with this cup your covenant of
grace and mercy. Amen.

Seventh Sunday After Epiphany

For the Bread

Accept us, Lord Jesus Christ, as we come to your table. We try to come as your responsive servants, wanting to learn here the ways of your love. As we break this bread together, we do so accepting your authority over our lives. Only your loving, forgiving grace can give our lives meaning and sense. We come before you seeking to learn. Teach us in these special moments of communion the way of your steadfast love, and teach us how to walk humbly in your way. Amen.

13

For the Cup

We bless you, O God, with all our hearts. As we
drink of this cup, we remember that all forgiveness, all health, all power is a gift from you, an
expression of your loving kindness. By your
tender mercies we find ourselves welcomed into
the presence of the living Christ. As you have
given the cold waters of spring to nourish the
ground and to satisfy all creation, so you have
given us a chance to drink of the living water of
faith in Jesus Christ our Savior. As we drink
from this cup of communion, accept the blessing
and thanksgiving we offer in your holy name.
Amen.

Eighth Sunday After Epiphany

For the Bread

God of deliverance and refuge, you are our rock
and salvation. In you we find strength and
shelter. You have kept your covenant with us.
You have rescued us from lonely exile away from
your Spirit. In this meal of communion, as we
break this bread that reminds us of Christ's body
given for us, we celebrate the love that never fails.
We accept now your covenant of love as our gift
to receive and our responsibility to share. Amen.

14

For the Cup

It is good to give thanks to you, God, to sing our praise to your name, O Most High. We rejoice in your steadfast love in the morning, your faithfulness at night. In all our hours, all our days, you are there. When we would forget this and become anxious and concerned for our own security, let this cup we share teach us the way of trust and commitment. Let this cup remind us that the love of Christ is constant and ever-giving, even to the point of death itself. Let this cup remind us to seek first your rule over our lives and to trust that all our other needs will be granted as well, in the fullness of your love. Amen.

Last Sunday After Epiphany

For the Bread

God of glory, we come into your presence with
awe and wonder. Your ways are beyond our
comprehension. Your glory is greater than that of
all the galaxies in the universe. Yet in the breaking of this bread, we can know you. For in it we
recall Jesus the Christ. We recall that Jesus came
to be our life and light, to lead us to your glory.
With Jesus at our side, we behold your glory not
with abject terror but with love and trust. In the
work of Jesus we have become your beloved
children and can answer your invitation to eat at
this table today. Amen.

15

For the Cup

God of light and love, hear our prayers. We get so caught up in the frantic routines of our days and in our own inner struggles that we fail to notice the wonderful ways your love is revealed to us. Help take the veil from our eyes so we can recognize your presence in our daily lives. Let us see in the common act of drinkinq together from your cup what it means to be part of Jesus Christ's body in the world. Let this act of communion help us see with new eyes your love and glory in our midst. It is in the name of Jesus Christ that we pray. Amen.

First Sunday in Lent

For the Bread

We remember today, our Creator and Provider, that we are always tempted to depend too much on ourselves and not enough on you. When we bake bread, when we earn our daily bread, we are tempted to forget that it is you who gives us bread. Teach us to remember and to stay faithful, as did your Son Jesus Christ when he was tempted in the wilderness. As we take this bread of communion, let us realize that we receive it from you. As we break this bread of communion, let our spirits be broken and humble, offered up to you. As we eat this bread of communion, let us be nourished and enriched by your everlasting love. We pray in the name of the one who was tempted, yet stayed true, Jesus Christ our Lord. Amen.

16

For the Cup

Dear God, we thank you that you are always there when we need you. Life so often seems like a desert, dry and confusing, full of mirages that appear to bring happiness. Yet when we run after these mirages, they shimmer and disappear. We thank you for your outpouring love, made visible in Christ's outpouring life, a life we commemorate and share in drinking this cup. We pray for your presence that refreshes and restores us, like a spring in the desert. Bless us with your presence in the dry places of life. In Jesus' name. Amen.

Second Sunday in Lent

For the Bread

We are your people, O God, gathered here at this table to be in covenant with you. We are Abraham's children, called to follow you in faith and trust. As we break this bread, let us be reminded that Christ's body was broken as a sign of your faithfulness. We would be faithful too. Strengthen us by this communion meal to stand firm in faith. Amen.

17

For the Cup

God our Creator, you have given us the very gift of life itself.

God our Redeemer, when we would wander like lost sheep, you have come to meet us and lead us back to the safety of your flock.

God our Host, you have welcomed us to the fellowship of your table.

God our Savior, your love is poured out for us like the blood of Christ was poured out, so that the covenant might be sealed and so that we might be yours.

For all the ways your love reaches out to us, touches us, welcomes us, we respond with thanksgiving. Amen.

Third Sunday in Lent

For the Bread

O God of those who have much and God of those who have little, as we see the bread on your table today as well as the bread on our tables at home, let us give thanks for all you have given us. Yet help us also remember that as we partake of bread, we are called to share bread. We must share bread not only with those around us, but with our sisters and brothers who are hungry. Let us share this communion around the world by sharing our offering. Amen.

18

For the Cup

As you have poured out your life-giving blood as a way of showing your great love for us, dear God, we continue in our gratefulness by the sharing of it in our fellowship. Show us ways we can share life-giving opportunities with others in your name. Amen.

Fourth Sunday in Lent

For the Bread

If we depended upon our own strength and virtue, O Lord, who could stand? Our foolish, self-seeking ways only drive us further from one another and from you. Yet you have reached out to us in Jesus Christ and led us from a far land to our true home. And you have prepared a banquet of celebration for us, a feast of hope at which we now gather. Here at this table we are reunited with you and with one another in a great feast of hope. As we break the bread here, we are reminded of the love of Christ, and we are welcomed home. Amen.

19

For the Cup

Our gracious host, you could have prepared for us a cup of fury, but instead you have poured out for us a cup of reconciliation. As we drink of this cup, and recall Christ's giving of himself for our sakes, we rejoice that the barriers that separate humanity from God are broken down. But help us find here also the courage, wisdom, and love to break down the barriers that separate us human beings from one another, so that we may be not only recipients of your reconciliation but ambassadors sharing your love to a divided world. In the name of the one whose cross broke down the walls of hostility we pray. Amen.

Fifth Sunday in Lent

For the Bread

Everlasting God, we cling to so many things. Those things in which we find our security become to us like chains. Our possessions act as burdens. Instead of serving us, they are served by us. In our frustration, we hear your call to hope, your call to freedom, your invitation to participate in a wonderful new creation. As we eat this bread, we do so in the wish that you would draw us away from being servants of dead things, so that we may better serve you, the living God. We pray in the name of the one who came as a servant of all, Jesus Christ our Lord. Amen.

20

For the Cup

As we gather in your name, we still remember
the beautiful act of sacrifice, devotion, and humility made by the woman who anointed Jesus'
feet with precious ointment. Her act of worship
remains as a model for us. It serves as a reminder
to us, as it did to Jesus, of the sacrifice that he
made in devotion and humility, pouring out his
very life for us. As we pour and drink this cup,
we accept the generosity of love you pour out for
us. Lead us. Teach us. Encourage us to follow a
lifestyle of giving and sharing the love of our
Savior. Amen.

Palm Sunday

For the Bread

Enter our hearts, O living Christ. We fling wide the gates of our defenses and our insecurity to welcome you. We shout our hosannas and proclaim our allegiance. Yet in the bright sunlight of celebration, there is a shadow—the cross-shaped shadow of testing and pain, humiliation and fear. As we come to your table this Palm Sunday, we ask that you give us faith and courage to *stay* loyal. As this bread reminds us of your loyalty to us, so let it reinforce us in loyalty to you when the cheering stops and we are put to the test. Support us in your love, O living Christ, as we share the meal you have given to us. Amen.

21

For the Cup

Center our spirits, O God of spirit and truth. On a joyous day of celebration, when your praise is so great that even the stones would cry out, quiet our hearts so that we may perceive Christ's coming, humble and meek, into our midst. As we drink from this cup of communion, let our attention be centered on the cup of suffering and death that you did not refuse, in order that we might drink from the cup of life and joy that you offer us now. Amen.

Maundy Thursday

For the Bread

Great God, you are the host as we gather in this special place to come to your table. We rejoice at this opportunity to share in this communion meal with people we know and love. Help us to realize that we are also in communion with our brothers and sisters in Christ in all lands. Help us to realize also that we are in communion with your good and faithful servants down through the ages who have been part of Christ's body, the church, and are now in the fellowship of saints. But most important, help us to realize that we break bread in communion with you and your disciples. That moment in a quiet, dark upper room happened only once. Yet in a real way it happens every time two or three are gathered in Christ's name. As we break this bread, send the Spirit of Christ to refresh us, to renew us, to restore us as followers of Jesus Christ. Amen.

22

For the Cup

Our loving God, you are the one whom Jesus Christ could call "Abba," Father. By Christ's example, we too can have the sense of being your children. We come to drink of the cup you offer on this holy night, remembering the words of St. Paul: "The cup of blessing which we bless, is it not a participation in the blood of Christ?" Help us to take these words seriously. Help us to be drawn into the reality of Christ's presence with us, of Christ's willing sacrifice for us. Help us to be true to the everlasting covenant that we reenact at this table. Keep us faithful to the Savior who suffered and died, so that we may rejoice with the Christ who has risen victoriously. Hear us as we pray in the name of the one who blessed the cup and who blesses our lives. Amen.

Easter Sunday

For the Bread

We give you thanks, O Lord, for you are good, and your steadfast love endures forever. As did the disciples of old, we felt lost from your love, and our fears drove us to hiding. Now we can cast aside the fears that once weighed us down, for Christ is risen and the death we feared most has lost its sting. In this bread, we remember the broken body of Jesus and the fact that you loved us unto death. Yet also in this bread, we find the food of our souls to nourish and strengthen us in the living Christ. As we eat this bread, we come out of hiding to tell the whole world that our Christ is alive! Amen.

23

For the Cup

Your love in Jesus Christ, O God, is a stone we once rejected because we were afraid that this giving, self-sacrificing love would lead us to death. But in the good news of the resurrection, which we celebrate this Easter Sunday, the stone that was once rejected has become the cornerstone of a temple that cannot be destroyed. For we have discovered that your love does lead us to death of self, but that it also leads us beyond this death to new life in Christ. In drinking this cup, we commemorate the love poured out for us at Calvary, but we also celebrate the conquering, everlasting, ever-living love of the empty tomb. In the name of the risen Christ we pray. Amen.

Second Sunday of Easter

For the Bread

O God of guidance and care, help us resist the temptation to set aside the joy and wonder of Easter and to resume the dull, safe routines of lives that aren't touched by your Spirit. Help us to remember that it is you we must obey, not the pressures of the marketplace or of social expectations. As we eat this bread, help us recall what Christ did for us. Help us accept our roles as royal priests, to draw the world to your love. Help us find the nourishment to serve you with faithfulness. We pray in the name of the one who was faithful to us, Jesus Christ our Lord. Amen.

24

For the Cup

We call upon your guiding spirit, O God, because we are helpless and confused before you. The news of resurrection, of new life in your love, is almost impossible to comprehend. Like Thomas, we suspect that it is too good to be true. We are almost afraid to believe the best, lest we be disappointed. In receiving this cup, help us realize that we are receiving your invitation to believe, to respond faithfully, to live in the power of new life, to say with our brother Thomas, "My Lord, and my God!" Amen.

Third Sunday of Easter

For the Bread

Good Shepherd, like helpless sheep we gather, needing your guidance. We hunger. We thirst. We are afraid. Like Paul, blinded on the road to Damascus, we need someone to take us by the hand, to heal us, to receive us into your community of faith.

We thank you for this table set before us, and especially for this bread; for in it we taste and experience the love, safety, and leadership of your fold. As we eat this bread, we are fed by the love of the one who is at once the Lamb of God and the Great Shepherd of the sheep, Jesus Christ our Lord. Amen.

25

For the Cup

At this communion table, O God, we are com-
forted; but we are also challenged. Like Peter, if
we are really to love you, we must feed your
sheep in our acts of love and witness. Like
Ananias, we must dare to love our enemies and
help lead them to your will. The cup you offer is
a cup of discipleship, a cup of service, a cup of
commitment, given in the shadow of the cross.
Help us to receive this challenge and accept it, as
we receive and accept this cup. Help us receive
your love poured out for us in Jesus Christ, that
we might love others in Christ's holy name.
Amen.

Fourth Sunday of Easter

For the Bread

Our dear God, we are members of your family gathered in this sanctuary, surrounded by the familiar faces of people we know and love. As we come to your table, we rejoice in this sense of being a family, of breaking bread together. Yet we need the aid of your Spirit to help us realize that your family goes beyond these walls. When we break bread here, we also break bread with people from every nation, from all tribes, peoples, and tongues who are one in Christ. Help us be sensitive to their needs, their hopes, their fears, even as we are to one another. In the name of the risen Christ who calls us to be one. Amen.

26

For the Cup

Lamb of God, you came among us in humility and quietness, and offered yourself up as a sacrifice. As we drink this cup, we ask to be purified by your love and healed by your mercy, that we might gather at the living waters with those who have conquered and say, "Amen! Praise, and glory, and wisdom, and thanks, and honor, and power, and might, belong to our God forever and ever! Amen!"

Fifth Sunday of Easter

For the Bread

Author of all love, we come together to be a part
of your loving community. It is in the spirit of a
loving community that we share this bread. In
taking this bread, in offering it up to you, in
blessing and breaking it, in sharing and eating,
we are imitating your Son and our Savior, Jesus
Christ. As we reenact this special meal, help us to
be more Christlike. Let our love for one another
be another way of following the example of our
Savior, that in the quality of our love, the depth
of our compassion, all people will know that we
are Christ's disciples. Amen.

27

For the Cup

O God of hope, there are signs of hope all around us—in the new births of nature during spring-time, in the daily renewal of our faith and lives, and in the living hope that is ours in Christ Jesus our Lord. Help us abide in your hope. Help us to trust in your love. Help us look forward to that time when all tears shall be wiped away and we shall live in the joy of your presence. Let this cup be an emblem of that hope that does not dis-appoint. As we drink from it, our hope is renewed, and so is our awareness of the trans-forming power of your love. Amen.

Sixth Sunday of Easter

For the Bread

God of peace, you have created us to be restless
and unfulfilled until we find our peace in you.
Help us be seekers of your peace, ambassadors of
your Spirit. Let us be quiet and responsive so
that your Spirit can speak to our deepest needs.
In these moments of communion, in this breaking of bread, we eat not by the world's standards
of what is satisfying, but rather by the grace and
peace of your sustaining Spirit. Amen.

28

For the Cup

You, O God, are our help in ages past, our hope
in years to come. All around us are precious
reminders of our heritage in faith. Symbols on
the walls and windows draw our spirits to you.
The symbols of bread and cup draw us into
deeper communion with you. Many of us asso-
ciate this place in our memories with special
moments in our lives, and it is like a home to us.
This meal is like a family dinner. But we know, O
God, that if all this were stripped away, and all
things of this earth that are comfortable, rich,
and rewarding were lost, your presence would
still be with us. Your world would be our temple,
and the glory of your love would be our light.
For in sharing this cup, we share the most
precious gift of all, the love you have poured out
for us in Jesus Christ. Amen.

Seventh Sunday of Easter

For the Bread

God of grace, God of power, the heavens proclaim your faithfulness, and all peoples behold
your glory. We come to your table today acknowl-
edging that the living Christ is Lord, our beginning and end, our morning star of hope and
promise. Help us learn of your love from this
bread. This bread can be broken and swallowed,
just as the body of Jesus was broken and
swallowed up by death. Yet this bread can
strengthen and transform our bodies, just as the
living Christ can strengthen and transform our
lives. We pray that, in this communion meal, we
will be reborn by your loving presence into the
new life of your Spirit. In Jesus' name. Amen.

29

For the Cup

O wonderful God, you are our vision, our life, our light. As we gather to drink from your cup, we will hold a physical symbol in our hands. We will see and feel the firmness of the vessel. We will see the sparkle of light on the juice it contains. We will smell and taste the juice's sweet sharpness. But our minds and souls will be drawn beyond these outer signs. In this cup, we will remember your life-giving love spilled out for us. In this cup, we will accept a new covenant to obey your commandment to love one another as you have loved us. In this cup, we will come to know Jesus Christ and the Father who sent him. In this cup, we will receive peace, not only as the world gives, but as God's Spirit alone can give. Amen.

Pentecost

For the Bread

We gather around your table, O Divine Host, led
here by your Spirit. It is only by receiving the
forgiving and reconciling power of your Spirit
working in our hearts that we would feel welcomed here. It is only in the discernment that
your Spirit brings that we would recognize Christ
in the breaking of bread. It is only in accepting
the power of your Spirit that we go forth from
this place with our lives refreshed and renewed.
Thank you and Amen.

30

For the Cup

God of power, empower us by your Spirit as we bless the cup you have given us in your mercy.

God of peace, as this cup is poured out, let your Spirit's peace pour out on us, and center our lives on the perfect peace that only you can give.

God of love, as we drink this cup, let us share it as your children, gathered in love.

God of hope, as we go forth from these moments of communion, let your Spirit remain our constant guide in life's struggles and our constant reminder that your love never fails, that we are never abandoned. Hear us, we pray, by your Spirit's help. Amen.

Trinity Sunday

For the Bread

Creating and creative God, we celebrate this
wonderful world you have made. Its beauty and
grandeur proclaim your glory and draw us to
praise its creator. Its harmony and order proclaim your wisdom and draw us to seek understanding. Its abundance and richness proclaim
your gracious providence, and call us to thankful
response. This bread we now break, grown from
the seed of grain by the light, rain, and soil you
have provided, reminds us of your mercy to all
creatures. It also reminds us of the ultimate
mercy, the ultimate promise of life given to us in
Jesus Christ, whose name we now bless. Amen.

31

For the Cup

God of guidance and light, we seek your Spirit's
leading. We seek to know as we are known, to
love as we are loved, to give as you have given to
us. As this cup is poured, we remember Jesus' life
being poured out in ultimate sacrifice, just as
your love has been poured into our hearts
through the presence of your Holy Spirit. In the
name of that Christ and that Spirit we pray.
Amen.

For the Sunday Between May 29 and June 4

For the Bread

Gracious and merciful God, our own virtues or attainments cannot make us worthy to come before you. We could never earn your love. Yet this bread is a symbol that you have made us worthy by first loving us. Give us the faith to accept your love and to let your healing and helping power work in us and through us, through the Spirit of the risen Christ. Amen.

32

For the Cup

God, you are the Good Shepherd who seeks the
lost and lonely. In the selfishness of our lives we
have wandered off and become strangers to you.
We have sought to please other people and do
what society expects, rather than to do your will.
Yet in your mercy, you provide for us and break
down the barriers that would separate us from
your reign. With this cup we celebrate that we
who have been far off have come near. We who
have been lost have been found. We whose lives
have been fragmented have heen healed. As we
drink, we celebrate your mercy and forgiveness.
Amen.

For the Sunday Between June 5 and 11

For the Bread

Where there is death, O living God, you can bring life. In breaking this bread of communion, we remember that when a grain of wheat is sown, it must die in order to grow a new plant containing many grains so we might have bread. We also remember that when your son Jesus Christ came, it was to die that we might know new life. As we reflect upon these mysteries, and as we reflect upon your body in eating this bread, teach us to trust that your power of life is infinitely greater than the power of death. Amen.

33

For the Cup

We lift this cup to be blessed by your presence, O God of life. As we pour it, as we drink from it, we remember the power of transforming life you have poured out to us in Jesus Christ. Help us have the faith to die to our old, selfish, self-righteous ways of life, and to live in the power of new life that only you can give. Amen.

For the Sunday Between
June 12 and 18

For the Bread

God of hope and courage, there are times when we feel that we are lost and that we have lost what is important to us. We aren't able to handle the pressures of life by our own strength, and we feel like giving up. Yet in the dry wilderness of such times, you come to us with nourishment and strength. More important, you bring to us the awareness that we are not alone. When we would have given up on you, we discover that you have not given up on us. Each week this bread of communion is a gracious reminder that in Jesus Christ you care and that you are there with us in all of life's struggles. Amen.

34

For the Cup

How good and precious it is that we can be here,
dear God, and drink of this cup together in
communion with your Spirit. We realize that we
could never earn the right to have this fellowship
with you, but that your love justifies us, and that
we in faith can accept the love you freely offer. In
gathering here and drinking together from this
cup of communion, we realize that it is only as
we live in Christ that we really live. Amen.

For the Sunday Between
June 19 and 25

For the Bread

God of light, God of truth, you have sent the
world Jesus Christ to reveal your light, to live
your truth, to show the way to your presence. In
breaking bread this morning, we realize that we
are a part of your community of faithful people
down through the ages. Let us find in eating this
bread the strength to be true to that heritage, to
continue being a light to the nations. In remembering the Christ whose body was broken for us,
help us realize also the presence of the living
Christ in our midst. Amen.

35

For the Cup

In sharing this cup you have given us through Jesus Christ, dear God, we are affirming our faith in the one who said, "Take up your cross and follow me." Help us to live up to this affirmation, that we may be your faithful people, one in the unity of the love poured out for us on Calvary. Give us, in drinking this cup, the guidance we need to follow your path, the strength we need to take up your cross, and the grace we need to be Christ's people in a difficult world. Hear us as we ask this in Jesus' name. Amen.

For the Sunday Between June 26 and July 2

For the Bread

The earth is yours, O sovereign God, and all its fullness, the world and all who dwell upon it. Our spirits dance in celebration and thanksgiving for your presence and power.

As we bless, break, share, and eat this bread, help it remind us that your love of humanity was so great that you became a human being in Jesus Christ and lived among us, healed the sick, suffered, died, and rose to new life. When we feel cut off, weak, and separated, let your Spirit give our spirits the persistence and courage needed to reach out in love and hope. On touching your presence may we find healing in our faith and love, and may we be given the power to live, serve, help, and heal in Christ's name. Amen.

36

For the Cup

You are the God of infinite glory, yet you emptied yourself to walk humbly in our midst. You are the living God, the source of all life, yet in the death of Jesus your life was poured out for us. You are the God of eternal power, yet you became weak, so that we, your weak servants, would know your love. It is in a spirit of thanksgiving and humility that we come to drink from your cup, to find the refreshment of spirit that only you can bring. Lead us as we drink of it to be dedicated in service to those among us who are weak and powerless, that we may follow the example of our Savior, Jesus Christ, who called us to share a cup of cold water to those who thirst. Amen.

For the Sunday Between July 3 and 9

For the Bread

You are great, O God, and greatly to be praised; your greatness is unsearchable. As we gather around this table to break bread, we realize our own brokenness. Our dreams and desires, our proudest accomplishments, lay defeated in life's dust. Our own internal conflicts tie us in knots and keep us from doing the right and the good. Yet thanks be to Jesus Christ, this bread also reminds us that Christ's life was broken to give us healing, that Jesus was delivered to death that we might be delivered from death. We come, called by the Spirit of the risen Christ, laboring and heavy-laden, knowing that Christ will give us rest. We come to take upon ourselves the yoke of the one who is gentle and humble of heart, casting aside the world's heavy burdens to receive Christ's yoke of love. Amen.

37

For the Cup

We praise you, dear God, and bless your name forever; for you are gracious and merciful, slow to anger, and your steadfast love abounds. From generation to generation, your great gift of love through Jesus Christ has been proclaimed and reenacted, as Christians have gathered around your table. Though languages, cultures, and centuries have varied, some things have been constant: Your cup has been raised, blessed, and shared, and the outpouring love of Jesus Christ has been recalled. When alone we are weak and fragmented; but when we gather around this table, receiving the blessing of your Spirit, we form a great chain of strength, mutual encouragement, and dedication to your will—a chain of love in which your power is made perfect in our weakness. Amen.

For the Sunday Between
July 10 and 16

For the Bread

God of creation, we praise your name as we
come into your presence this morning. We realize
that our wisdom is but foolishness compared to
the beauty and power of your word, that our
greatest generosity is stingy compared to your
self-giving love. In your wisdom and love, you
have given us the living bread of Christ Jesus, the
bread that gives eternal life. As we eat this physical bread this morning, help us realize that our
true bread, our true source of life, is the living
presence of Jesus Christ. May your Spirit guide
us. Amen.

38

For the Cup

You are our true wisdom and true word, O God of Jesus Christ. In you and you alone can we find life, meaning, and sense. As your word took on human flesh and your love was poured out like the wine from this cup, so we have been able to receive this life you have so freely given. Thank you for this cup and for the wisdom of self-giving love that stands behind it. In Jesus' name we pray. Amen.

For the Sunday Between July 17 and 23

For the Bread

How often, our God, do we eat the bread that does not satisfy, when instant gratification of manufactured needs brings empty hearts and empty lives. We thank you that now we are invited to eat the bread that does nourish, the sustaining bread of communion with our Lord Jesus Christ.

Strengthen our spirits. Encourage our wills. Renew our strength. Guide us by your Spirit, that we may travel lightly in the world, unburdened by the weight of worry and possessions, so that we may bring healing and health, and that we may spread the good news of life abundant in Jesus Christ our Savior. Amen.

39

For the Cup

Your gifts of love are overwhelming and overflowing, O God of grace, and we thank you. You
are our creator and sustainer, and the source of
all our joy. Where there is the gall and bitterness
of stagnation and death, you pour out the wine
and honey of life. This cup we now pour reminds
us that in the spilling of the blood of Jesus, there
was death, but that out of that death came
unstoppable, abundant life. As we drink this cup,
seal us by your Holy Spirit, that within our lives
and through our actions your steadfast love and
your faithfulness may find expression, that your
righteousness and peace may kiss. Amen.

For the Sunday Between July 24 and 30

For the Bread

God of time and eternity, you are the first and the last, the beginning and the end. We thank you that in our short lives, we reflect a glimmer of your eternal life; that in our feeble love, we can comprehend your infinite love; that in our hesitant and imperfect giving, we can imitate your perfect grace. We break this bread in order to share it, in order to act out the message of Jesus Christ and his self-sacrificing love. We recall when your disciples, faced with a hungry crowd, had only a few loaves and fish. You challenged them to share; they responded, and a great multitude was fed. We have few resources, and the world is hungry. Yet you challenge us to give of what we have in faith. As we eat this bread of communion, may we be empowered by your Spirit to share what we have in order that it might be multiplied by your love. Hear our prayer in Jesus' name. Amen.

94

40

For the Cup

You are the one God, and we thank you that you have called us to oneness with you and with others. When we drink this cup, we are reminded that in Christ's self-sacrificing love all the barriers that would separate us have been broken down. Because of Christ on the cross, your love has proven stronger than human fear and hostility. When those times come in which we do feel separated from your love, empower us by your Spirit to ask for and receive your holy love. Then enable us to break down the barriers that separate others from you, so that we may affirm around your table of love that we are indeed one in Christ's Spirit, around the world and forever. Amen.

For the Sunday Between July 31 and August 6

For the Bread

God, our gracious host, we love your holy name. We thank you that you work with those who love you for the good of all creation. As in Jesus Christ you fed multitudes with a bread beyond price, so we now come to you—hungry, asking for the bread of inner peace, the bread of strength and courage, the bread of hope. We pray for the peace, strength, and hope that your Spirit can give, so that we may live the kind of life to which we have been called; a life of gentleness, patience, love, and service, as befits followers of Jesus Christ. Amen.

41

For the Cup

When we would fall, O faithful God, you catch and lift us once again. When our spirits are low, your Spirit gives us encouragement. When we hunger for your presence, you hear our cries and fill our needs. How thankful we are that you care!

We raise this cup today, recalling our Savior's last earthly meal and remembering the supreme love expressed therein. We drink this cup as one. Help us to live, work, and witness as one, bound together in love by your Spirit. Amen.

For the Sunday Between August 7 and 13

For the Bread

Gracious God, you have provided us with what we need, but we so often hunger for that which does not nourish, that which does not fulfill our deepest needs. Help us to accept the words of Jesus when he said, "Do not labor for that which perishes but for the food which endures to eternal life." When we hear this invitation, let us accept the claim that Jesus is the Bread of Life and find in him the nourishment we need. Thank you for this bread we now eat, and the relationship it symbolizes. Amen.

42

For the Cup

Sometimes, O God, our lives seem dried out, shriveled up, and parched of meaning. It is only when we turn to you, the wellspring of joy and love, that we can be truly refreshed. There, your Spirit gives us new life, transforming our inner deserts into gardens. Thank you for this cup, given to us by Jesus Christ our Lord, a cup that represents new life, and life abundant. Let this cup remind us to turn to you for the refreshment and renewal of spirit we so desperately need but so rarely seek. We pray in the name of Jesus who invites us to this table of joy. Amen.

For the Sunday Between August 14 and 20

For the Bread

How thankful we are, O gracious God, that you give your children bread! Your children wandering through the desert received manna. Elijah the prophet was sustained in the wilderness. The spiritually starved people of Jesus' day heard him say, "I am the bread of life." We, too, come to receive your sustaining presence in the breaking of this bread.

Let us be nourished, strengthened, heartened, and encouraged by this breaking of bread. As you have shared with us, let us learn to share with the world the bread of life. Here we learn that only in sharing is there true living. Amen.

43

For the Cup

We come seeking you, our God, and we realize that here you have found us. We come looking for a sense of your love, and we realize here that you have loved us before we were ever born. We come as lost, beaten-down prodigals, seeking only forgiveness, and you rush out to meet us and to welcome us home.

How wondeful are your ways! How wonderful it is that we can drink of the cup of your unending love and receive your tender forgiveness! As we refresh our souls at your banquet, lead us by your Spirit to respond to others. Let us imitate the way you have responded to our needs—with kindness, forgiveness, and mercy to those whose lives we touch. We pray in the name of the Christ, whose cup of forgiveness we drink. Amen.

For the Sunday Between August 21 and 27

For the Bread

Provider God, you have given us a rich earth that yields to us its abundance. You have blessed us richly. As we eat this bread, we offer it up as a symbol of your care and providence in supplying us with our earthly needs. Yet even more, as we break this bread, we remember that the body of our Lord Jesus Christ was given for us. We claim the promise Christ gave that in receiving the living bread, we receive your promise of life. Yet help us not be content just to receive your rich blessings, but let us give generously of that which brings life. Amen.

44

For the Cup

How grateful we are, O God of peace, for this sense of communion with you through Jesus Christ. We remember the blood of Christ our Savior as we drink this cup, and we marvel at so great a love that would lead Christ to die for us. As we seek and find here the inner peace that your presence can bring, we would also heed your Spirit's call to seek peace and pursue it—in our families, with our neighbors, in our churches, our community, our nation, and our world. Let us find at this communion table the strength and courage to be makers of peace, keepers of justice, doers of righteousness, followers of Jesus Christ. Amen.

For the Sunday Between August 28 and September 3

For the Bread

Dear God, so many voices seek our attention and our loyalty—television, advertisements, clubs, parties, good causes. They all want some commitment, some investment from us. Your call, your invitation, is different. You want our loyalty, too, but you have first given us yours. As we break this bread. we remember vividly the cost of your loyalty to us—the broken body of Jesus Christ. As we eat this bread, we receive the strength we need to live for you. Amen.

45

For the Cup

This cup, O God, reminds us that Christ's life
was poured out for the world, that we might
receive life. We thank you for the church, your
community of faith, the vessel that receives and
shares the life you have poured out. Fill us now
that we might be emptied in loving service.
Amen.

For the Sunday Between September 4 and 10

For the Bread

The bread is broken, and once again we are guests at your table, Lord. It is here that we can taste and feel the bread in our mouths, and realize how real is your love for us. As we enjoy the hospitality of your table, help us to cherish these moments of communion. Sustain us as we attempt to live for you and in your Spirit in the week ahead. Amen.

46

For the Cup

Dear God, we stand in awe and wonder when we consider the sacrifice Jesus Christ made on the cross—that his body was broken, his blood spilled, that we might know your life and love. As we come to this table and remember, in the drinking of this cup, your great sacrifice, we offer to you our sacrifices—our weak bodies, our divided minds, our broken spirits. We know that you can take us in our brokenness and transform us into a living sacrifice, good and acceptable, that Christ's love may be seen in our daily lives. We pray in the name of the one whose cup we drink. Amen.

For the Sunday Between September 11 and 17

For the Bread

O merciful God,
When you have wanted us to be childlike, we have been childish.

When you have wanted us to cooperate, we have been competitive.

When you have wanted us to lift one another up, we have torn one another down.

When you have wanted us to be peace-makers, we have stirred up conflict.

Yet this communion table is to us the sign that your love never gives up; your patience never gives up; your forgiveness never gives up. In eating this bread, we who are so often weak find the strength we need to try again to live as you would want, following Jesus Christ. Amen.

47

For the Cup

Here we gather at your table, gracious host, realizing that the ordinary values of our world are here turned upside down. Here we gather not according to rank and power but in humble service. Here we gather not in terms of seniority and prestige, but in our ability to be childlike. Here we gather not in trust of our own abilities, but in trust of your steadfast, unconditional love. Let this cup be the symbol of that love, a love poured out on Calvary. Let our willingness to drink of it be a symbol of our willingness to follow you in humble service and childlike love. In the name of Jesus, who blessed the children, we pray. Amen.

For the Sunday Between September 18 and 24

For the Bread

Our God, you are our light and salvation, and our safe refuge from all that we would fear. In Jesus Christ, who courageously faced the cross, you taught us that perfect love casts out fear. We delight in coming to your house, filled with the beauty of your love, to share at your table in the bread of iife. Help us to realize that this bread symbolizes the coming of Jesus Christ into our midst, to show us the way of love and sacrifice. Teach us to follow Christ's example and to walk in meekness and humility. We pray in the name of Jesus Christ. Amen.

48

For the Cup

We come to drink the cup of mercy, knowing we have received your mercy when we had wandered far from your presence. We come to drink the cup of forgiveness, because it helps us recall that the blood of Christ is the perfect sign of your willingness to forgive. Yet, O merciful God, although we are glad to receive your forgiveness, we are often reluctant to forgive others. Help us to learn not to pass judgment on our brothers and sisters, but to forgive and show mercy. In sharing this communion cup, we affirm that you have planted the seeds of love and forgiveness in our hearts. We pray that you will water these seeds, that we might harvest right relationships and peace with others as servants of Jesus Christ. Amen.

For the Sunday Between September 25 and October 1

For the Bread

You hear us when we cry to you, O God of steadfast love. You are gracious and answer us. You have invited us to seek your presence, and you have not hidden your face from us. In Jesus Christ we have looked upon your goodness and glory, and have been received as your children— even as your friends. In this bread we now bless and eat, we affirm this mystery: that you were once in our midst in human flesh, and are even now in our midst by the power of your Spirit. Bless us as we partake, and let the living Christ work in us and through us. Amen.

49

For the Cup

God of light, your glory fills the universe as the waters fill the sea. Your power and majesty are beyond human comprehension. Yet in Jesus Christ, you willingly poured out your glory, power, and majesty. You emptied yourself, becoming a humble, obedient servant. As this cup is poured out, we remember that the life of Jesus Christ was poured out for us. As we drink this cup, we confess that this Christ whose life was poured out is now the risen Lord, who reigns in glory. We pray that we may learn at your table to pour out our love for others in true and humble service, so all the glory may be Christ's. Amen.

For the Sunday Between October 2 and 8

For the Bread

Our God, in Jesus Christ you are the great shepherd of the sheep, leading your lost and confused people to green pastures and still waters. We come to the table that you have spread before us, grateful to be in your life-giving presence, sharing in the richness of your love. As this bread we now break fills our minds with the knowledge that Jesus Christ is truly in our midst, we pray that Christ's joy and peace may fill our hearts. Help us to realize that the joy and peace we receive here is real only as we are willing to share with others what we have received. We pray in the name of the gracious host who invited us to this banquet, Jesus Christ. Amen.

50

For the Cup

Dear God in heaven, your steadfast love has led
and blessed your people through the centuries.
We come to your table in loving trust, praying
that we might give glory to Christ. As we taste
life in drinking this cup, we realize that Jesus
tasted death for everyone. Help us to become
more dedicated to your will and your way,
following the example of Christ, who lived out
the message that to be great, we must serve; that
to find life, we must be prepared to lose it in
Christ's service. Amen.

For the Sunday Between October 9 and 15

For the Bread

Gracious God, your kindness is hard for us to understand. Our days are few, and our flesh is weak; yet you are eternal, and your name endures forever. We are selfish and prone to aggression; yet you are tender and forgiving, and you offer us a peace that passes understanding. In breaking this bread, we realize the price at which this peace was given and the ultimate depth of your love through Jesus Christ. Help this meal to be for us a banquet of peace, a meal of reconciliation, a feast of joy. Help this feast transform us into living parts of the body of Christ, serving, giving, and loving in Christ's name. Amen.

51

For the Cup

From everlasting to everlasting, you are God. Your love lasts longer than the mountains; your compassion is vaster than the galaxies of space. The cup we now lift for your blessing is a sign of your compassion, for it reminds us that the lifeblood of Jesus Christ was poured out for us. As we drink from this cup, help us to remember that because Christ died, we live. Although we remember Christ's death, we worship a Christ who is alive and who gives to us the power of life. We pray that you will dedicate us to be your loving, serving people. Amen.

For the Sunday Between October 16 and 22

For the Bread

When we have been prisoners to our own fears, you have set us free. When we have been blind to the needs of others, you have opened our eyes. When we have been low in spirit, you have lifted us up. When we have hungered, you have given us bread. Let this bread of communion remind us, O God, that you provide for our deepest needs, that in the presence of Jesus Christ we have found our nourishment and strength. Help us remember, gracious God, that as you have met our needs, it is for a purpose. You want us to be your people, bringing freedom, light, hope, and bread to the world around us, as ambassadors of Christ. Amen.

52

For the Cup

Because of your work of reconciliation in Jesus
Christ, dear God, we can come with confidence
to your throne of grace with the assurance that in
your presence we may receive mercy and find
grace. We can trust your word because you sent
Jesus Christ into our midst, as one who came not
to be served but to serve; to offer his life as a
ransom for many. As we bless this cup and drink
from it today, we remember that Jesus said, "The
cup that I drink you will drink." In so recalling,
we realize that we come here in the joyous
union of your love, but also that we are called to
go from here in dedication and service. Strengthen
us to your service. Amen.

For the Sunday Between
October 23 and 29

For the Bread

O God, our comforter and guide, you have done great things for your people, and we are glad. In Jesus Christ you have led us from an exile of the spirit to new life and new hope. We come now to the table that Christ has set, accepting Christ's invitation as part of Christ's family. Bless us in our lives as this bread is blessed. Heal the broken places of our lives and relationships as this bread is broken. Sustain and nourish us as this bread is eaten. We pray this not just for our own needs, but that we may better serve your will and more faithfully follow your way. Amen.

53

For the Cup

This cup is a cup of love poured out for us, O giver of life and love, for it represents the life of Christ that was poured out for us. In drinking this cup, we celebrate your eternal, ultimate, self-giving love, and offer to you our love with all our hearts, souls, minds, and strength. Remind us that, as we drink this cup, we drink it with our neighbors here and around the world. Remind us that if we are to love you fully, we must love our neighbors as we love ourselves. Bring us together now in the perfect unity of love to which Christ has called us and with which your Spirit seeks to bless us. Amen.

For the Sunday Between October 30 and November 5

For the Bread

God of peace, we pause in the midst of busy and anxious lives to come into your presence and partake of this communion meal. Teach us with the psalmist that unless you are with us, it is vain to "rise up early, to go late to rest, eating the bread of anxious toil." Still our hearts. Center our minds. Quiet our anxious spirits, that we may know your peace. Let the bread we now eat strengthen and nourish us so that all our daily bread, and all our daily work, may be sanctified by your presence. We pray in the name of the one who is our bread of life, Jesus Christ. Amen.

54

For the Cup

You are the one true God, and we come into
your presence with prayer. We lift this cup before
you, seeking your blessing upon it, and seeking
your Spirit to be poured out into our lives. Let
these moments of communion be moments of
renewal and rededication for us, so that our
dreams and our days may be filled with your
presence. Give us grace to turn away from the
false gods of success and security, in order that
we may love you with all our hearts, souls, and
strength. We pray in the name of the one who
supremely trusted you and lived out your love,
Jesus Christ. Amen.

For the Sunday Between November 6 and 12

For the Bread

God of Justice, we come to break bread before you. Help us realize your special care for those who hunger, those who are oppressed, those who are powerless and cast aside. Help us remember that this bread is a bread of judgment upon our complacency and contentment. Help us to realize that we have received your compassion so that we may be able to give compassion to others. Let this symbolic act of sharing bread at your table call us to the task of sharing bread with the hungry, of bringing freedom to the oppressed, of sharing power with those who have none. As you shared with us in our need, help us to share with others in their need. In the name of the compassionate Christ we pray. Amen.

55

For the Cup

When we look upon the richness of the grace
that has been poured out upon us, we can see our
spiritual poverty, O self-giving God. We can give
nothing by comparison to what you have given
us! This cup we now lift reminds us of all your
good gifts of life, but especially of Jesus Christ,
whose love was poured out from the cross. Let
this cup of communion teach us to trust in your
love's sustaining power, and to share your love
with others. Teach us the secret of your grace,
that it is in giving we receive; in emptying
ourselves in humble service that we become filled
with your love. Teach us that whatever we can
offer is transformed by your love into a grace
that can change the world. Amen.

For the Sunday Between November 13 and 19

For the Bread

Gracious and merciful God, you are slow to anger and abounding in steadfast love. You are good to all, and your compassion extends over all creation. Because of what you have done for us in Christ Jesus, we have the assurance of your goodness and confidence in your love. Because of Christ's body, broken in sacrificial love, we see that your love will endure forever, that you are faithful. Help us to break and to share this bread in faithful response, holding fast to your promise. Let your compassion work through us, that our lives of service may be seen as living and acceptable sacrifices. We pray in Jesus' holy name. Amen.

56

For the Cup

In these moments of silent communion, eternal God, we pray that the noise and clamor of our daily lives may be stilled; that the insistent demands placed upon us by our hectic schedules may be silenced; that our ears, our hearts, and our spirits may be receptive to you. In listening and waiting silence, we prepare our hearts, trusting that you are here, that you are active in our midst, that you make the ultimate difference in life. We wait upon you to bless this cup, to enrich our lives by helping us to remember Jesus' dying sacrifice; to be aware of Christ's living presence; to have the hope that the future is Christ's and that Christ is in our future. We pray in the name of the Sun of Righteousness that shall rise with healing in its wings, Christ the risen Lord. Amen.

Last Sunday After Pentecost

For the Bread

In our attitudes, in our actions, in our desires, and in our fears, we are like sheep who have strayed far from the green pastures and still waters. We cry out in our need; and because you are the Good Shepherd, you hear us, seek us out, and rescue us in the scattered places to which we have wandered. The bread we now break is the symbol of your shepherd's care; for you feed us, you guard us, you protect us, you seek and find us through Jesus Christ. Dedicate us to your will as we partake of this bread of communion, that we may truly be the sheep of your pasture, responding to the needs of the world around us as you have responded to ours. We pray to you in Christ's holy name. Amen.

For the Cup

In Jesus Christ you have revealed yourself to us,
O God, as the Alpha and the Omega, the
beginning and the end, who was, and is, and is to
come. We come into your presence now, seeking
to share in communion with the one true God.
This cup we lift before you is the cup of reconciliation, a visible reminder of the love that holds
all things together. In drinking this cup, we
acknowledge the fullness of your presence in
Jesus Christ and in Christ's dwelling among us.
As you have made peace between earth and
heaven by the blood of Christ's cross, help us
become peacemakers here on earth. Let our
words, our service, our action, our giving—all be
witnesses to the world of the love you have
poured out for humankind in Jesus Christ, our
Lord and Savior. Amen.

Index of Scriptures

This index contains references to biblical passages either quoted, paraphrased, or used as the basis for an idea in a prayer or set of prayers. References preceded by a (B) indicate passages used in the prayer for the bread. A (C) indicates a passage used in the prayer for the cup. No designation indicates a passage used in both prayers in a set. The number following a reference refers to the number on the upper right hand corner of each prayer.

133

Topical Index

(B = Bread; C = Cup)